SOUTHERN ELECTRICS

Volume II

1948-1972

The Post-War Builds & Locomotives

Kevin Derrick

Strathwood

First published 2020
IISBN 978-1-913390-07-5

Copyright Strathwood Publishing 2020
Published by Strathwood, 4 Shuttleworth Road, Elm Farm Industrial Estate,
Bedford, MK41 0EP. Tel 01463 234004
www.strathwood.co.uk

Contents   Page

4-SUB 'Shebas'

Opposite: Setting off towards Shepperton from Raynes Park on what looks like a glorious day is 4105 with a mid-morning service via Wimbledon on 4 August 1961. Although the Bulleid designed prototype 4101 had gone into service during October 1941, the restrictions of the war years meant that construction of the remainder of this batch did not recommence until late 1944, with units 4102 to 4110 going into service during the following few months into and early 1945.
Colour Rail

The first of this real production batch 4102 is seen faithfully plying its trade near East Dulwich on 16 May 1963. The accommodation within these units was compartment only throughout. They went into service first on the Eastern Section and were familiar across all of the London suburban routes by the 1960s.
The Bluebell Museum Archive

Towards the end of its working life on 25 July 1969, 4110 has the 12.50 lunchtime departure from Waterloo via Brentford Central for Hounslow as the motorman coasts towards Isleworth station passing Wood Lane Crossing signal box. As a local lad, your author spent many a happy hour watching trains at this location at this time. *John Scrace*

Likewise now in green with a full yellow end, 4107 draws into Richmond a few weeks earlier on 12 July 1969 heading for Teddington and then back towards Waterloo on a Kingston roundabout service. Another out and back Waterloo to Waterloo service is seen within the great London terminus on 25 October 1969 as 4106 prepares to head towards Hounslow via Richmond and return via Brentford Central.
Both: Strathwood Library Collection

Snaking its way back into Waterloo during the late summer of 1970 we find 4104 having returned after a trip around the Kingston roundabout. To maintain a more comfortable temperature inside the compartments as usual most have their windows down on a warm day. *Colour Rail*

Opposite: Putting in another appearance this time at Clapham Junction on 19 September 1969, 4107 is bound for Balham this time. The nickname of Shebas arose from a biblical reference towards squeezing as many people in as possible within these units compartment design. *Chris Nash*

On 28 December 1971 just before it was withdrawn 4106 gets away from St. Margarets towards Twickenham with another Kingston roundabout service.
Colour Rail

To help with a shortage of suburban stock in 1969, two additional 4-SUB units 4131 and 4132 were created from spare trailers and ex 2-HAL power cars. Seen at Victoria, 4132 was created from 2637 & 2688 and two trailers from 701 the shortlived 7-TC. Whereas 4131 seen arriving at Crystal Palace, was made up from 2622, 4282, 701 and 2659. *Both: Strathwood Library Collection*

With the shortage now overcome, the pair break their journey towards the scrapyard of King's at Wymondham in East Anglia with a stopover here at Feltham on 2 April 1972, having been stripped of their pick-up beams and as many spares as was thought prudent. *Colour Rail*

Opposite: The first of the more numerous all-steel design of 4-SUB units went into traffic in April 1946 numbered 4111. This next batch as far as 4130 were put into service in their latest style of Southern Railway livery still worn by 4118 just after Nationalisation around 1948 when seen at London Bridge. *John Aston*

The Post-War 4-SUBs

After much criticism from passengers having to scramble over each other's feet within the confines of the earlier compartments of 4-SUB units, later builds enjoyed the use of open saloons, as indeed would their passengers. In winter use both the compartments and the open saloons could become like saunas inside during wet and snowy weather with so many passengers bringing in moisture to be quickly heated up by the often very efficient electric heating units underneath the seating. Unit 4653, when seen at Beckenham Junction, carried the earlier style of British Railways crest in this view from the 1950s. *John Aston*

Another of the early all compartment 4-SUB units 4117 appears to be in first-class order as it stands at Norbiton in the late 1950s while working on the Kingston loop.
John Aston

One oddball unit was 4590 which ran for a short while in this form with two all-new steel vehicles from 1950 until disbanded in March 1956. On 6 April 1953, it caught our cameraman's attention at the rear of this service at New Cross.
Richard. C. Riley/The Transport Treasury

Construction of the all-steel 4-SUB units ran until 1951. The breaks in their number series allowed for the augmented pre-war units described in the companion volume. However, the later units with open motor coaches along with the original one open trailer and one compartment trailer as built would enjoy longer service lives as many units became reformed to allow the phasing out of older compartment stock, which in later years were more prone to vandalism. Both the later and earlier styles of set numbering can be seen here with 4630 at Gipsey Hill on 18 October 1959, and the earlier version as S 4714 at Waterloo East with a Dartford to Charing Cross service.

Photos: Richard. C. Riley/The Transport Treasury & John Aston

The earlier British Railways crest gave way during the latter part of the 1950s on the EMU fleet to the universally used coach style of roundel. Here we have 4626 arriving at Clapham Junction and then 4691 and a companion 4-SUB arriving at Raynes Park with a Hampton Court service around 1960.
Colour Rail & Rail Online

During off-peak times units would be separated and stabled at several locations to reduce wear and to allow for cleaning. The former L.S.W.R. terminus here at Hampton Court provides us with an example of this on Sunday 2 December 1962 as fellow enthusiasts walk back along the platform having just seen off a steam special. *Colour Rail*

As the 1960s progressed yellow warning panels began to adorn the Southern Region's large fleet of EMUs, just before the next change of colour scheme to the new blue livery, we find an ex-works 4741 arriving at Clapham Common with a stopping service from Victoria bound for Coulsdon North towards the end on the summer of 1966. Another view taken a few weeks later shows the first built of the all-steel 4-SUB units 4111 leading a duo of 2-BIL units at Woking as part of a Victoria to Brighton semi-fast service. *Both: Colour Rail*

Opposite: A real mix of livery variations among both types of Post-War 4-SUBs are to be found laid up in between the morning and evening peak hours here at Crystal Palace in 1969. Liveries vary with green and blue with both small and full yellow ends and a Sheba 4102 for good measure. **Derek Whitnell**

Forming a Reading-Waterloo line semi-fast for a change 4734 disgorges some passengers at Winnersh Halt. *Mike Morant Collection*

The first few 4-SUB units into blue such as 4154 were sent out with the smaller white coach and set numerals along with smaller InterCity arrows than those later adopted as standard, this view was taken near Wimbledon on 21 August 1967. *Colour Rail*

The future for fire damaged 4282 at Micheldever around 1969 looks bleak now. Along with 4381, they both carry the extra handrails above the motorman's windows as they do not open to allow the route stencils to be changed compared with 4125 seen opposite at Waterloo on 27 April 1971. West Croydon plays host to 4381 on this occasion with the 16.38 Victoria to Sutton on 5 May 1970. **Photos: Chris Nash & John Scrace**

The Tin HALs

Opposite: This formation snaking away from Victoria on 9 June 1969 has 2-HAL 2698 bringing up the rear. *Colour Rail*

Left: The corridor side of 2695 has the lead in this view of the 08.08 Portsmouth to Brighton on 5 September 1970 at Worthing. *John Aston*

Below: Likewise, 2698 makes another appearance on 27 July 1968 at Crawley leading the 10.40 Bognor Regis to Victoria. *John Scrace*

A number of all steel vehicles were built to replace collision and war-damaged casualties such as 2-BIL units 2014, 2102, 2119 and 2131 and 2-HAL 2646 and to provide some additional stock towards the close of 1948. Seven new 2-HAL units numbered 2693 to 2699 entered service on the Eastern Section at first, as the new 2-HAP units arrived, later on, these 2-HALs were cascaded onto the Central Section. Although they were perhaps cruelly nicknamed as the Tin Hals, they provided both additional seating and luggage space which saw them being favoured on the ends of Gatwick Airport services.

All seven units survived to be painted in the later blue livery, with units 2693 and 2695 also being seen with full yellow ends for a while still in green livery. As newer stock arrived onto the Brighton line during the mid-1960s they were being used elsewhere within any 2-HAL and 2-BIL combinations, although perhaps less so on the Reading lines. The first unit withdrawn was 2693 in the summer of 1970, the remainder dropping out of traffic during 1971.

One additional unit was created in 1954 numbered 2700, the Driving Trailer Composite being built upon the frame of the damaged former 2-BIL 2014 and the Motor Brake Second came from 4-SUB 4590 seen on page 15. The DTC leads here in this view taken at Fratton on 3 April 1960, the unit was disbanded in March 1968 with the DTC being formed into 2-HAL 2688 and the MBS into 4-SUB 4369. *The R.C.T.S. Archive*

Four further Driving Trailer Composites were created between 1949 and 1953 to replace damaged vehicles within 2-BIL units 2069, 2100 and 2133 and also for 2-HAL 2653.

The Double Deckers

Just after the end of the Second World War, there was an upturn in the passenger numbers on the Dartford Loop. The usual solution of lengthening trains would be a major problem on this route due to the considerable infrastructure expenditure that this would entail. Tasked with finding a solution using double-deck trains within the Southern's restricted loading gauge called upon some blue-sky thinking from Oliver Bulleid and the drawing office staff at Lancing Works. As a result, two double-deck units coded as 4-DD and numbered 4001 and 4002 were built during 1949. Ten years later on 12 June 1959, we see the pair arriving at Cannon Street. *Richard C. Riley/The Transport Treasury*

An interesting early photograph of both of the units on test early in 1950 at Charing Cross, several modifications had to be made to the units before they were passed ready for service. At this point, they are painted in malachite green with larger set numerals being used at first.
Strathwood Library Collection

Both units were given their second major overhaul at Eastleigh Works during 1965, they returned to traffic now fitted with new roller blind route indicators to replace the original stencil style, these were strangely picked out in white when 4001 was seen at Guildford on test, also now adorned with small yellow warning panels.
Colour Rail

The double-decked duo is seen next being led by 4002 at Waterloo East with an up service from Dartford in July 1969. Both sets having now been given full yellow ends at Selhurst depot during January 1968. *John H. Bird/www.Anistr.com*

Both units were based at Slade Green depot for regular maintenance. Typically they were put onto two of the busiest duties from Dartford into the capital each morning Monday to Friday. During the day they would either run solo or be stabled back at Slade Green. The evening commuter turns would see them paired up once again for an average of three return runs out and back along the Dartford route. This would be a regular sight for city workers still during July 1969 as 4-DD 4001 leads 4002 at Waterloo East with a rush-hour Charing Cross to Dartford train. in July 1969. With a second view showing 4002 bringing up the rear at the same location.
Both: John H. Bird/www.Anistr.com

33

Although they were capable of moving large numbers of passengers, it came at a cost as they took longer to get on and off the trains and accidents sometimes occurred as the sets did not have footboards or commode handles. The pair are seen at Charing Cross on 22 June 1970 with a route to Slade Green showing on 4002's blinds. The change into blue livery was made at Selhurst during September 1970, along with new numbering as 4901 and 4902. This last view taken during June 1971 is once again at Charing Cross. Their last ever working was reported as being the 18.04 Charing Cross to Dartford via Bexleyheath on 1 October the same year. *Photos: **Colour Rail & John Vaughan/Rail Photoprints***

4-EPB & 2-EPB 1st and 2nd Series

Several of the Eastern Section's fleet of 4-EPBs are prominent in this view of Slade Green Depot on a sunny 8 November 1958. The first unit numbered as S 5001 went into service in January 1951, photographically they were ignored to some extent in favour of other railway subjects at the time. Which means that portrait shots such as the one opposite of 4-EPB 5021 at London Bridge in April 1955 are now quite rare.

Photos: Richard C. Riley/The Transport Treasury & John Aston

Durnsford Road Power Station helps to supply the juice to these two 4-EPB workings as 5024 is about to be overtaken by an eight-car rake on the down fast line in this view from 2 March 1957.
Richard C. Riley/The Transport Treasury

Opposite: The many new changes to the layout around Petts Wood are being surveyed by one interested passenger looking out from 4-EPB 5105 as it forms what appears to be a Cannon Street to Orpington service around 1960. *Rail Online*

As we have seen already in Volume I many of the older 4-SUB vehicles and their augmentation trailers would go towards the manufacture of the 4-EPB fleet during a time when there was a national steel shortage just after World War Two. Construction of the 4-EPB fleet brought about numbers 5001 to 5053 being introduced from 1951 to 1954 and 5100 to 5260 going into service between 1953 and 1957. A still-new S5258 complete with the otherwise abandoned S prefix stands alongside 4-SUB 4330 at Cannon Street in 1957. The rainstrip above the doors was one of several modifications within the build of the fleet as seen on S5213 setting out across the River Thames from Cannon Street on 30 May 1958. *Photos: Colour Rail & Richard C. Riley/The Transport Treasury*

A splendid view taken from a privileged visit to the signal box overlooking Charing Cross station shows a spread of 4-EPB units at the terminus on a very cold 3 December 1958.
Richard. C. Riley/The Transport Treasury

The livery for the 4-EPBs when introduced was officially in malachite green, this gave way later to a darker shade due to re-varnishing and or repaints into the later dark green paintwork. The appearance of 5010 at Datchet on the Windsor & Eton Riverside branch around 1964 is enlightened with the yellow warning panel. *Strathwood Library Collection*

Passengers turn their backs on 4-EPB 5041 forming the 16.58 Hayes to Cannon Street service as it arrives at London Bridge on 31 July 1963. As elsewhere the spread of the new blue livery would leave its mark across the 4-EPB fleet as the 1960s further progressed, with one of the earliest examples being 5219 arriving at Clapham Junction on 4 February 1967, on a Waterloo to Effingham Junction working.
Photos: The R.C.T.S. Archive & Colour Rail

The second series of EPB vehicles were closely aligned to the standard British Railways Mark I coaches. Taken on the last day of steam services on the Westerham branch, 4-EPB 5303 complete with the early style of experimental integral air horns to either side of the driver's windows races past Dunton Green on 28 October 1961. These 4-EPBs were constructed between 1960 and 1963 in the series 5301 to 5370. *Peter Simmonds*

Both 5305 and its 2-EPB cousin 5744 from the 5701 to 5800 series have the preferred top-mounted air horns in this view at West Croydon. *Rail Online*

The construction of so many 2-EPB units not only allowed the Eastern Section to run ten-car trains with the use of 4-EPB sets to help with increased passenger loadings on many routes but also provided for a few services that could barely justify a single 2-EPB set as here at Selsdon in 1963. *Rail Online*

Opposite: Similarly a number of the earlier design of 2-EPB units were constructed to match the earlier EPB outline in 1959, these were numbered 5651 to 5684 and became regulars on the Waterloo to Windsor & Eton Riverside route as here with the 13.38 service bound for the capital making a stop at Datchet on 18 April 1968. *John Scrace*

The 2-HAPs

Opposite: Making up a six-car set as the blue liveried 2-EPB 5655, mates up with the green liveried 4-EPB 5121 to form the 12.38 Windsor & Eton Riverside and the 12.33 Weybridge to Waterloo which joined up at Staines as they make their stop at the rarely photographed Southern Railway opened commuter belt station at Whitton on 20 September 1969. *www.TOPticl.com*

The 2-HAP units were very similar to their 2-EPB counterparts except they were designed for mainline services rather than suburban use, as such express gear ratios were fitted. They also had 1st class accommodation and toilet facilities. Two batches were supplied from 5601 to 5636 between 1957 and 1959, then 6001 to 6173 between 1957 and 1963. Here we see 6055 running as part of a Margate service on 27 September 1963 at Ashford. *Colour Rail*

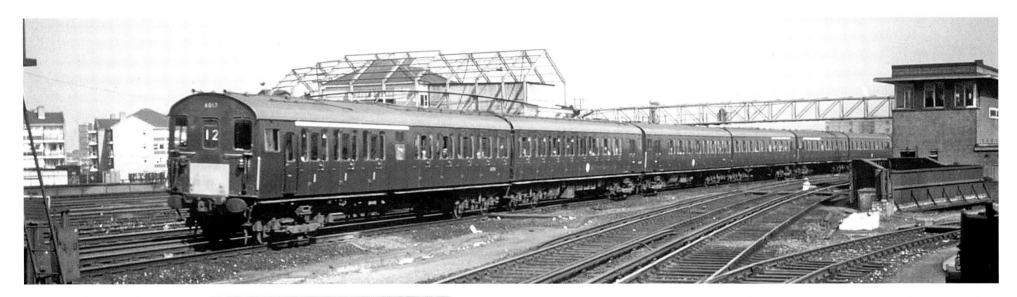

An eight coach Victoria to Brighton semi-fast made up from 2-HAP units led by 6017 swings into Clapham Junction during September 1966. *Colour Rail*

On 16 November 1970. The Driving Trailer Composite from what looks like an ex-works 6167 has come to grief here at London Bridge. *Andy Gibbs Collection*

Opposite: A ten-coach 2-HAP rake heads down the Portsmouth line led by 6140 at Woking on 30 October 1966. *Colour Rail*

The CEPs and BEPs

Opposite and this page: The large repair shops at Chart Leacon are seen during a conducted tour in the early 1960s with 4-CEP 7162 having some attention to its leading bogie, while 2-HAP 6078 is in for maintenance alongside. The 4-CEPs and 4-BEPs were introduced between 1956 and 1963 firstly to take on the major express workings as part of the Kent Coast electrification scheme alongside the 2-HAP units on the semi-fast services. The passage of a Dover Marine express lead by 4-CEP 7125 gives one of the station porters at Tunbridge Wells good reason for caution as it speeds through in the early 1960s. *Both: Rail Online*

In 1956 six prototype units were built for testing on the Central Section, four of them were formed as Motor Brake Second Open (MBSO), Trailer Composite Corridor (TCK), Trailer Second Corridor (TSK) and another (MBSO), their 4-CEP coding was around them being Corridor EPBs. Likewise, two 4-BEP units were Buffet EPBs with a Trailer Buffet replacing the (TSK). Both of these views show 4-CEP 7102 in the late spring of 1955. *Both: Strathwood Library Collection*

Further batches of both 4-CEP and 4-BEP were built between 1958 and 1963 supplied to both the Eastern and Central Sections along with a few for the Western Section. These sets were not noted for good riding qualities, as such the final deliveries were made with the more efficient Commonwealth design of bogie. The number series for the 4-CEPs being from 7101 to 7211 and the 4-BEPs were from 7001 seen here near Dorking in late 1967 up to 7022 in their number series. *Colour Rail*

Although the through corridor concept was similar to the 4-COR design from the 1930s in some ways, except the head code box was now placed within the corridor connection. When the 4-CEP units were new many were sent for storage before the Kent Coast electrification scheme went live, this resulted in eighteen 4-CEP units being stored at one point on the Ardingly to Horsted Keynes line all in one long row stretching for just under a mile in length. On 2 June 1966, 7126 has just arrived at Victoria from the south coast. *Colour Rail*

The then-new blue livery applied to 4-CEP 7107 tucked on the back of this service passing Hildenborough Junction around 1967 caught the attention of this cameraman. *Colour Rail*

The first units in service were painted in malachite green, progressing to darker green repaints then with small and full yellow ends later on. One or two units were also seen in the early blue livery with small and with full yellow ends as here on 7211 in the latter livery seen below arriving at Balcombe on the 14.43 Victoria to Brighton on 13 June 1970. Finally, they all settled into the blue and grey InterCity livery. *John Scrace*

A chance for some fond farewells on the platform just before departure time as 4-CEP 7139 is in the then-new and fashionable InterCity blue and grey livery on 14 September 1968, with a soon to depart Dover service from here at Victoria. *Derek Whitnell*

Miscellaneous

During 1964-1965 the first batch of 4-CIG units numbered 7301 to 7336 were delivered along with with the 4-BIG buffet car fitted equivalent units 7031 to 7048. Still, in as-delivered condition, 4-CIG 7302 brings up the rear of this service heading for Victoria passing through Clapham Junction in September 1968. *Chris Ralls*

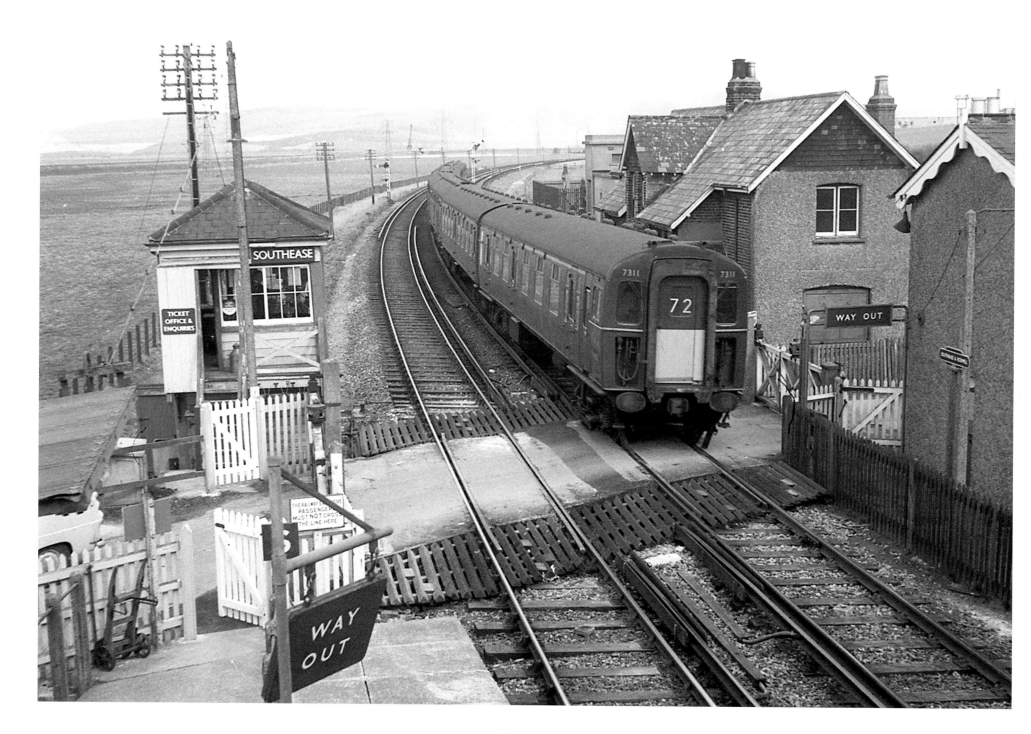

Opposite: This first flush of green liveried 4-CIG & 4-BIG units were put to work on the Central Section where we see 7311 arriving at Southease & Rodmell Halt, with a Seaford train on 4 March 1966. *Peter Simmonds*

The similarly styled 4-REP and 4-TC units for the Western Section and the Bournemouth electrification, in particular, were introduced soon after but in the then-new plain blue livery complete with alloy InterCity arrows. An up service arrives at Southampton Central on 10 June 1967 made up from 4-REP 3009 with 4-TC units 410 and 404. A few weeks earlier on 15 April 1967, it is E6047 providing the power for this rake of 4-TC units led by 411 just south of Clapham Junction with the 12.35 service to Bournemouth.
Both: Strathwood Library Collection

Things have gone wrong today in the very busy station throat at Waterloo on 11 July 1968 as this 4-REP and 4-TC combination has managed to split the points, forcing the power to be switched out while the mess is sorted out. The crane and breakdown gang do their best to get everything back to normal while a Class 74 has the missing vehicles from the 4-REP to hand in the background. *Andy Gibbs Collection*

The last of this type of 1963 designed stock to arrive were the 4-VEP units as effectively vestibuled EPB units using the Mark I coach styling. Whereas the 4-CIG, BIG, REP and TC units were primarily for express workings, these 4-VEP units with their additional doors and higher density seating were for semi-fast and outer suburban services. The first twenty units 7701 to 7720 were delivered during 1967, the latter of which is seen here upon delivery at Clapham Junction the same year, being put into service on the Bournemouth line in their overall blue livery coupled with small yellow warning panels and those stylish alloy InterCity arrows. The passengers also had bright orange curtains (fashionable at the time) fitted to shield them from unwanted sunlight on all of these units. *Rail Online*

As further batches of 4-VEP units arrived from BREL at York after 1967 they were put into service with full yellow ends as displayed by 7728 arriving at Littlehaven on 10 July 1971, with the post rush hour 18.36 Victoria to Horsham semi-fast. The overall blue livery by this time was being rapidly replaced with a blue and grey livery for all semi-fast stock. *www.TOPticl.com*

Opposite: During March 1968 the three new 4-VEP units 7739/41/42 were formed into this 8-VAB unit which included a buffet car to supplement the services on the Bournemouth line. We see it at Stewarts Lane during June 1969, although it was repainted in blue and grey livery before it was disbanded in 1974, it only allowed 4-VEPs 7741 and 7742 to be formed at last as some vehicles within the 4-VEP fleet had been damaged in accidents. *Jonathan Martin*

Not strictly a Southern electric perhaps, but the first of the Eastleigh Works built Motor Parcels Vans although destined for the North Eastern Region on Tyneside, first underwent its trials on the Southern, as we see here hauling a good rake of passenger stock departing Redhill on 24 November 1955. It was numbered as E68000 and took up service on the South Tyneside route in March 1956. With the Kent coast electrification looming, it was also thought desirable to introduce ten similar vehicles (Motor Luggage Van or MLV) for the Southern, these were additionally fitted with batteries for working into the dock areas at Dover and Folkestone away from the third rail, as demonstrated here by S68009 at Folkestone Harbour during September 1961. *Photos: The Bluebell Museum Archive & Colour Rail*

An interesting and busy shot taken at Faversham on 21 April 1968 as one of the MLVs in green livery leads one of the then-new Trailer Luggage Vans or TLV on a Dover Marine to Victoria via Chatham & Catford Loop boat train. Selhurst depot converted six of these TLVs numbered S68201 to S68206 during 1968. Within a few years, all of the stock seen in this train would be in blue and grey livery, but for now, it was to be seen in green, blue & grey, green, blue and blue & grey again to the rear of the CEP and BEP units in the train. *Strathwood Library Collection*

An interesting view of the shortlived 7-TC unit while still running as 900 taken at London Bridge on 13 May 1966. This unit was formed using the driving coaches from 2-BIL unit 2006 after it was disbanded in June 1963 to create a testbed towards push/pull operation with Class 33 locomotives along with additional passenger capacity on the rush hour services on the Oxted line. The original 2-BIL jumper cables were altered to connect with the B.R.C.W. built Type 3 locomotives. The unit was renumbered as 701 before it was disbanded early in 1969. *Colour Rail*

A further 6-TC unit was converted at Eastleigh Works in early 1965 from coaches drawn from disbanded 4-RES motor coaches and trailers from 6-PAN and 6-PUL units. It was turned out in green with a small yellow warning panel and numbered as 601. Like the earlier 7-TC 900 it was used on the Oxted and East Grinstead route initially with the first of the pul & push adapted B.R.C.W. Type 3 locomotives D6580. We see it out on test at Salisbury after an overhaul at Eastleigh in August 1967, outshopped in a fresh coat of blue paint. *Colour Rail*

With its work completed as a testbed for the Bournemouth electrification and onward workings to Weymouth, 601 settled into use on the Clapham Junction to Kensington Olympia shuttle service being worked just like a conventional set of coaches. In June 1969, it was Class 33 D6555 diagrammed as the motive power when seen at Kensington Olympia, this service was known to some as the Kenny Belle. *Rail Online*

The unit was involved in a minor buffer-stop collision at Kensington Olympia on 16 June 1970 which resulted in 601 being set aside in Clapham Yard before being towed here to Micheldever for possible repairs the following month. On a visit on 10 January, 1971 to Micheldever 601 was keeping company with 4-SUB 4292. The 6-TC was condemned officially on 9 October 1971. *Gordon Edgar/Rail Photoprints*

An earlier visit here to Micheldever in 1966 found not only 4-COR 3137 awaiting tripping and entry to Eastleigh Works for an overhaul but also several ex-London Transport tube stock vehicles for adaption and use on the Isle of Wight to eliminate steam services. A seven coach test train is seen at Clapham Junction in September 1966, the rear 4-VEC set is already in blue livery with a full yellow end, whereas the 3-TIS set nearest awaits a repaint. Six sets of each were created and took up service on the island from 20 March 1967. *Photos: Strathwood Library Collection & Rail Photoprints*

Litter

o trains

A busy scene at Ryde Pierhead on 4 August 1970 as passengers avail themselves on an, unfortunately, cut back network as an electric service on the Isle of Wight now. *Ian Nolan*

The Southern Region already had a taste of underground tube stock with the English Electric 1940 stock for the Waterloo & City Line built at the Dick Kerr & Co. Works in Preston. There were twelve Motor Open Brake Seconds like S62 seen here probably at Lancing, there were also sixteen Trailer Open Second cars entering service in October 1940. Due to its wet nature, the route deep below Waterloo's ex-L.S.W.R. terminus was known to many Londoners as "The Drain". *Strathwood Library Collection*

Another resident of the Waterloo & City line down in the depths for most of its life was DS75. This Siemens built electric locomotive was delivered in 1898 to work coal wagons which had to be brought down in the Armstong Lift to supply coal for the electric generator station. As with the passenger stock the air braking was charged from a static supply here at Waterloo. These two 1950s views show both ends of this locomotive which worked here until 1969 when it joined the National Collection of preserved locomotives. *Both: Colour Rail*

In 1901, a second, more powerful electric shunting locomotive was acquired for the Waterloo & City line as a standby, also to have the ability to rescue failed passenger trains in the tunnel if required. It was designed by the L.S.W.R.'s Chief Mechanical Engineer, Dugald Drummond. During 1915 it was brought back up to the surface and put to work shunting up the steep incline to deliver loaded coal wagons into the company's Durnsford Road Power Station supplying the then expanding suburban electric railway network. Perhaps often seen by enthusiasts from their passing trains working along the mainline for over forty years, but seldom photographed up close, DS74 is a rare beast on film, just like its subterranean cousin DS75. We have two views of it here, firstly while still in service during the early 1950s at Durnsford Road in Wimbledon and again inside Brighton Works about the time of its withdrawal and scrapping in 1961.
Photos: Strathwood Library Collection & Colour Rail

The Boosters

Combining their talents Oliver Bulleid and Alfred Raworth set about overcoming the gapping problem faced by third rail electric locomotives with the use of large flywheels and generators within the locomotives to act as boosters when the power was lost. This led to the three locomotives 20001 to 20003 later as Class 70 being nicknamed by some as Boosters while others knew them as Hornbys after the train set company. The first locomotive numbered as CC1 was built at Ashford Works in 1940 and carried these speed whiskers in a grey livery for its first two years before being repainted the same as CC2 to the left in malachite green. We can also see the bow pantagraph for use in sidings which were planned to be wired on the overhead system. The second locomotive CC2 also carried more marker lights at the expense of the route stencil originally fitted on CC1 above. *Both: Strathwood Library Collection*

The original Southern lettering changed to read British Railways in 1948 retaining the attractive malachite green livery but now numbered as 20001. This had now given way to black livery complete with a silver relief stripe when 20001 was spotted with a special passing Streatham on 3 June 1951. *Richard C. Riley/The Transport Treasury*

Opposite: Our next view of 20001 from 7 March 1960 while it was stabled outside at Stewarts Lane shows the livery now in a darker locomotive green with an off-white and a red lining stripe, white window surrounds and that rather industrial and hefty looking solebar being painted black. Also of note is that the stencil headcode box has been plated over since our last view. *Rail Photoprints*

83

A customary seasonal rain shower greets 20001 in our next view at Newhaven Town station on 10 April 1963. The air operated warning whistle remains alongside the driver's window and the white faces of the route indicator rings show up well too. *Ian Nolan*

Aside from a change of livery to blue complete with full yellow ends in time for working H.M. The Queen's annual Epsom Derby race special on 29 May 1968, this view which was taken at South Croydon also shows the additional roof-mounted horns and the removal of the route indicator lights and their replacement with a new headcode blind box which took place in April 1967 during a visit to Eastleigh Works. *Colour Rail*

This frontal view of 20001 was taken on 4 January 1969 during a stop at a rather foggy Lewes, this was while running the Bulleid Pacific Preservation Society and L.C.G.B. organized Sussex Venturer Rail Tour. It also shows that the headcode route blind box was fitted off centre, both 20001 and 20002 had been posted as withdrawn on 22 December a few weeks beforehand with 20001 specially reinstated for this run. Seen underneath the overall roof around this same time we catch our last view of 20001. It was stored with 20002 in Brighton's Top End Yard until 6 July 1969 when the duo headed for Cashmore's scrapyard in Newport where 20001 had been cut up by the end of the following month.

Photos: Strathwood Library Collection & Colour Rail

Opposite: We pick up the story with 20002 as she emerges ex-works from Brighton on 20 June 1951. Before this, she was reported as carrying an experimental light blue livery and exhibited to the Railway Executive at Kensington Addison Road during 1948. When introduced new from Ashford Works in 1945 the livery was malachite green as we saw on page 81, certainly 20002 still carried this livery at Nationalisation with the Southern lettering changed to read British Railways early in 1948. *The Bluebell Museum Archive*

Our next view finds 20002 ex-works once again but this time at Eastleigh in May 1959. The livery has changed to locomotive green with off-white solebars and window surrounds, grey roof, red buffer beams and red and white lining. Allocations for both 20001 and 20002 were the same, starting their British Railway's careers based at 75A Brighton, from November 1948 they were notionally allocated to Durnsford Road in Wimbledon, then officially to Stewarts Lane from March 1959, returning to Brighton from August 1966 until the pair were withdrawn at the close of 1968. *Colour Rail*

A general coat of grime has toned down the paintwork on 20002 when we catch up with her next at Victoria on 24 April 1962. The grey painted roof is now totally lost as a result. She has also gained overhead warning plates affixed to her flanks and front end for those rare occasions she worked under the Southern Region's overhead. *R.C.T.S Archive*

Another works visit to Eastleigh sees her in a slightly lighter green livery, with black solebars, silver roof panels and red buffer beams but no lining. She has also lost the external route marker lights in favour of a new headcode indicator box, and the whistle has been joined by air horns. *Colour Rail*

Opposite: Regular turns for the Boosters would be on Victoria and Newhaven boat trains as here at Clapham Junction by the 1960s. In earlier days they had seen regular use on heavy freights on the Central Section, sometimes their power and turn of speed would leave their steam-powered bankers wheezing along in their wake on these duties. *Rail Online*

On 30 June 1966, 20002 finds employment on a south coast parcels and mail train pausing here at Hove. We can see from the front end in this view again the new headcode box is offset, also that the whistle is still present along with roof-mounted horns and even at this late date still no yellow warning panels applied! *Ian Nolan*

Our final view of 20002 was taken at Eastbourne on 12 July 1967, whereas we can see that the yellow warning paint has finally caught up with this locomotive. However, all of the overhead warning plates have disappeared now. *R.C.T.S. Archive*

The third locomotive 20003 was built at Brighton Works and released for trials in September 1948. The design was changed and as a consequence, it weighed six tons more than its two sisters 20001/2. The original livery as seen here at Victoria on 15 May 1949 upon its arrival from Newhaven was in malachite green with cream lining and lettering. *Rail Photoprints*

As part of an impressive line up of modern motive power at Eastbourne which included the Fell locomotive 10100 at the opposite end to the freshly repainted 20003, this was laid on to impress visitors here to the International Union of Railways' Conference in June 1951.
The Bluebell Museum Archive

After a few years, the black livery had given way to lined green in the same style as her sisters, however in this scene under a stormy sky at Eastleigh in May 1959. Her paintwork certainly needs refreshing along with any repairs during this next overhaul, also she now does not carry a British Railways crest on this side at least. *Colour Rail*

That last repaint has added both crests and overhead warning plates, while the solebars have been turned out now in black in this next view at Stewarts Lane in the early 1960s. *Strathwood Library Collection*

Another early 1960s scene of 20003 stabled in the sunshine between duties this time on the spur at Three Bridges, all three of these electric locomotives would be soon classified as Class 70. *Colour Rail*

A rare view of 20003 soon after its front end was cleaned up by removing the external route marker lights and replacing them with new two-digit headcode route indicator boxes. Also, roof-mounted horns have been fitted, while the painters have simplified the livery with no lining anymore and sending her back to work as here at Newhaven Harbour around 1966 without even a small yellow warning panel in place.
Strathwood Library Collection

Our final view finds 20003 stabled with 20002 within Brighton station on 7 May 1967. She was placed into store at Brighton during September 1968 to await repairs, however, she was soon posted as withdrawn instead on 6 October. After a period of storage at Durnsford Road, she was sent to George Cohen's scrapyard at Kettering to be scrapped in the autumn of 1969. *Strathwood Library Collection*

Class 71

An official view of E5000 soon after this Doncaster Works built locomotive entered service out of 73A Stewarts Lane on 24 December 1958. This example would go on to enjoy three renumberings and a full rebuild within its short seventeen-year service life. On 1 December 1962, it was renumbered as E5024, which it carried until withdrawn in October 1966 when it was set aside for conversion into Class 74 E6104. It next returned to traffic from Crewe Works on 25 February 1968 as an electro-diesel, renumbering into TOPS as 74004 took place during December 1973. This was shortlived as it was withdrawn for good this time on 31 December 1977. It then found its way to Bird's Commercial Motors at Long Marston for breaking up. A rare view from above in a passing train over Stewarts Lane on 5 April 1959 allows us to see those seldomly used pantographs. Notice also how E5000 has its numbers placed closer to the cab windows than E5004.

Photos: Strathwood Library Collection
& Richard C. Riley/The Transport Treasury

Two glimpses of the freshly delivered E5003 and E5004 in 1959, having just arrived from Doncaster Works they await acceptance testing at Eastleigh Works before being released into traffic and sent to Stewarts Lane for driver training. In February 1967, E5003 was set aside to join the Class 74 electro-diesel conversions, becoming E6107 upon release from Crewe Works on 31 March 1968. Whereas E5004 retained its identity until renumbered as 71004 in January 1974. *Both: Colour Rail*

When this modern motive power show was put on at Battersea, E5022 was the latest arrival of the class and was chosen to take part. Here she is on 9 October 1960 underneath the mock catenary next to E3056 which in reality would need a supply of 25kV AC rather than E5022's requirement for 650v DC. Classified as HA by the Southern Region, E5022 would be renumbered as E5006 on 13 October 1968 to fill the void left after the original E5006 became a Class 74 as E6103. *Colour Rail*

This photograph of E5003 and E5019 stabled on their usual spur at Stewarts Lane around 1962 conveniently shows both sides of the locomotives. E5019 would also go on to later become another of the Class 74 conversions emerging as E6105 on 10 March 1968. *The R.C.T.S. Archive*

We believe E5012 is being prepared here at Neasden shed in May 1961 to be put on display as part of a large exhibition soon to be put on in Marylebone's goods yard by the Institute of Locomotive Engineers. *Strathwood Library Collection*

With a heavy draw of current through its traction motors, E5015 sets off up the short but steep climb up Grosvenor Bank out of Victoria to cross the River Thames with a heavy rake of Pullman cars dragging behind her on 14 May 1961. *Colour Rail*

Two days later on 16 May 1961, the preparation E5015 for the down Golden Arrow is more in keeping with Stewarts Lane standards of the time as they near Great Chart. *Colour Rail*

Something of a regular for use on the Golden Arrow now she is clean and tidy as E5015 gets another run on this once prestigious service again in July 1961 as they clear Saltwood Tunnel near Folkestone. This example was set aside in October 1966 to become E6101 upon a return to traffic as a Class 74 out of Stewarts Lane on 11 February 1968. *Rail Photoprints*

First introduced into traffic on 8 December 1959, E5013 had visited here for a light overhaul when seen at Eastleigh Works on 7 October 1961 being repainted into a darker shade of green and losing its lining in the process. *Colour Rail*

Photographed within Eastleigh Works around 1963, this close-up shows the positioning of the numbers for all of the class at this time, save for E5000 and as we see here it kept the same higher number placement when it was renumbered as E5024 on 1 December 1962. On 27 July 1963, as E5024 it was keeping company with E5012 in the sunshine at Stewarts Lane.
Both: Strathwood Library Collection

Another visit to Stewarts Lane in 1963 finds E5003 popping up once again still carrying its original lining while another class member behind it has now lost its lining after an overhaul.
The R.C.T.S. Archive

In May 1963 on a further visit to Stewarts Lane, it's the turn of E5008 to stand sentinel outside the shed building. This example became 71008 in December 1973 to run until finally withdrawn in November 1977, after fifteen months of previous storage at Chart Leacon beforehand. *Strathwood Library Collection*

Sweeping around the curve at Aylesford under clear signals E5017 puts some work in for the railway with this fitted goods in August 1963. This is another locomotive destined to become a Class 74 a few years later as E6109 on 28 April 1968.
Rail Photoprints

The headboard may well be in place but the lack of flags and the cleanliness of E5010 here at Dover Marine in the mid-1960s suggests standards have certainly slipped from a few years before. *Colour Rail*

Signs of a recent overhaul with its new plain green livery adorn E5020 running light through Chichester on 29 April 1964. This locomotive would be renumbered as E5005 on 31 October 1968 while already running as E5020 in the new InterCity blue livery, this was to fill the void left after the original E5005 had become E6108. *Colour Rail*

On 7 March 1965 at Stewarts Lane, E5018 keeps company with E5019 in between duties. On 15 December 1968, E5018 also took up a new number this time of the vacated E5003, whereas E5019 had by then been rebuilt into E6105 and sent back into traffic on 10 March 1968. *Rail Photoprints*

An ex-works portrait of E5011 outside in the sunshine at Eastleigh on 11 September 1965, ready for traffic once again. *Colour Rail*

Porters busy themselves stowing passenger's luggage before this morning's down Golden Arrow departs Victoria on 24 September 1965, thankfully the side brackets on E5017 are being put to good use today for displaying those splendid gold painted arrows. *Colour Rail*

The Southern Region was perhaps slower than all of the other regions in adopting yellow warning panels to many of its locomotives, both to its many B.R.C.W. Type 3 diesels and to these HA electric locomotives too. Here we have a mid-1960s shot of E5009 ready for undergoing testing to its pantagraph in this secluded area of Eastleigh Works. Another view of sister locomotive E5010 taken at the same location on 23 April 1966, once again shows a lack of yellow paint. Ironically in the background, we can see an ex-works Sulzer Type 2 being turned out with a yellow panel for another region! *Both: Rail Online*

Again here we are later in 1966 on 21 September at Ashford in Kent, just as E5021 rolls a fitted freight from Feltham via Hither Green on the down through road, while E5018 lurks in the background without any warning panels as yet either. Very soon E5021 was to be set aside in May the following year for conversion into E6110, while E5018 would later become E5003 in 1968. *Colour Rail*

No actual date was given for this shot of E5013 at Dover Marine but we estimate it to be either 1967 or 1968. *Rail Online*

When the yellow panels finally did appear on the green locomotives, their size and shape varied as with E5014 passing Shoreham Lane in Orpington with the Night Ferry in June 1967. *Colour Rail*

Once again updated in a different style but most likely during late 1967, it will soon be departure time for E5007 at Victoria. This example was noted still without any yellow panels in March but then also noted outshopped in blue by May of 1968 (see page 130). Also noted carrying this slightly wider style of a yellow panel covering the side marker lights was E5009. *Rail Online*

Throwing a few sparks from its collector shoes as it heads through Clapham Junction on 28 September 1966 we can just make out that E5023 has gone the full monty with regards to yellow ends before going into the blue livery. This would finally come only after it was set aside in January 1967 once converted into a Class 74. It returned to traffic in this guise as E6106 on 17 March 1968, based out of Eastleigh. Others of the Class 71s known to have run for a while in green livery with full yellow ends were E5001 and E5010 during 1968-69. *Colour Rail*

Opposite: The first of the class to make it into blue livery appears to have been E5004 in the spring of 1967 when it is seen that September she is set to work this morning's down Golden Arrow away from Victoria. Renumbering into TOPS as 71004 came in January 1974, she was set aside into storage at Hither Green on 3 October 1976 where she would stay until 21 June 1979. A brief period of being dumped in Temple Mills Yard followed until 23 July when her passage to Doncaster Works took place for scrapping along with 71009/10/11/13 and 71014. *Rail Online*

The side brackets for the golden arrow embellishments show up well in this view of E5007 enjoying the sunshine outside the shed at Stewarts Lane on 30 May 1968 soon after being repainted into blue at Eastleigh Works. The larger size of the new style of numbers forced them to be positioned behind the cab doors from now on. *Strathwood Library Collection*

Opposite: A further variation in the pattern of yellow warning panel is worn by E5012 seen at Orpington in June 1968, Also E5001 was in this style for a while too before going to a full yellow end. Modellers are well-advised to consult a dated photograph as we have noted at least five variations in the shapes of these warning panels. *Colour Rail*

We believe that E5010 was the last example to remain in green livery, here she is at Tonbridge on 25 October 1969 with a Minster to Thurrock goods. Certainly, by late May 1970, E5010 was turned out in blue from Eastleigh Works after an overhaul and back into traffic once again.
Strathwood Library Collection

Ready for departure away from London Bridge during February 1969 with a van train we find E5008 without any headcode showing, therefore, its destination remains a mystery. The end for this locomotive would come in the Newport scrapyard of John Cashmore in the autumn of 1978.
John H. Bird/www.Anistr.com

Class 73

Below: Ironically the second locomotive E6002 went into service without the benefit of yellow warning panels in a plain green livery also with a roundel. In this scene, the locomotive is on test under its diesel power in the works yard at Eastleigh in early March 1962. *Colour Rail*

Opposite & above: As there were too many sidings to fit overhead wiring to on the Southern Region it was decided a compromise or hybrid of a reasonably powerful electric locomotive with a moderate diesel engine capability to work away from the juice could be a very useful addition to the fleet. Eastleigh Works went ahead and produced six locomotives classified as JA with E6001 being the first into traffic on 1 February 1962. This undated view of the locomotive coupled to D6559 at Dover Marine is we think a crew training and clearance testing run soon after it entered service. The second view on this page shows E6001 at Stewarts Lane in April 1966, the repaint from its first overhaul has now seen the size of the yellow warning panel reduced slightly and the addition of grey and white relief body lines while still retaining the roundel carriage style of British Railway's crest.
Photos: Colour Rail
& Strathwood Library Collection

We next find E6002 at Ashford on 26 August 1964, now having gained grey and white bodyside reliefs to the sides only, but no yellow warning panels as yet, although they would come soon afterwards in the same wider style as E6001 on the previous page. *Colour Rail*

Opposite: Among the locomotives on display at the Eastleigh Works open day in August 1962 was E6003. It had entered service on 27 April and was the first to carry the grey and white relief bands. Likewise, the slightly wider yellow warning panels would later appear. *Ian Nolan*

Next into service out of Stewarts Lane depot would be E6004 on 6 July 1962, now with round buffers, this view at Slade Green was taken soon afterwards. Again E6004 was later to be seen with the wider yellow panels before its later repaint into the standard blue livery. *Colour Rail*

Opposite: Another subtle difference can be seen on E6005 here at Stewarts Lane in 1963 as the grey for the centre roof panels has also been extended across the cabs. By this stage an order for thirty production locomotives had been given to English Electric at their Vulcan Foundry, this would soon be increased further to forty-three new electro-diesels. *Strathwood Library Collection*

The final prototype JA electro-diesel E6006 entered service on 15 November 1962. For a short while in late 1965 until 1967-8 before these prototypes were repainted into plain blue they could be seen alongside the first few of the production locomotives which were now known as Class 73. This is E6006 on shed at Hither Green around this time, while opposite E6007 in its early blue livery was to be found alongside the last few weeks of steam workings into Bournemouth on 17 June 1967. *Both: Colour Rail*

The first of these production locomotives E6007 went into traffic on 10 October 1965 with the final one E6049 joining the fray on 15 January 1967. Some rudimentary cleaning was being carried out on E6010 alongside D6511 at Hither Green on 4 January 1966. Also seen on this same visit was the brand new E6011 showing off the grey painted roof and side grills when new, note the lack of any InterCity arrows up to this example, Whereas the next E6012 would get them from new.

Rail Photoprints & The R.C.T.S. Archive

Providing the motive power for a rake of brand new 4-TC units in June 1967 at Southampton Central is E6012 with an up service for Waterloo. Full blue livery for this Class 73 would come in August 1969 after an overhaul at Eastleigh Works. *Colour Rail*

The grey and white bodyside relief band was dropped from the production series from E6014 onwards, leaving the remainder to emerge from the Vulcan Foundry in the style of E6037 seen here at Wimbledon soon after its delivery on 3 July 1966. *Colour Rail*

Having arrived into service on 30 October 1966, we see E6047 propelling this Bournemouth service at Basingstoke on 31 March 1967. Sister engines E6035 and E6012 are seen outside the shortlived diesel maintenance shed that was erected at 70B Feltham in January 1967 alongside the soon to close marshalling yard. *Both: Colour Rail*

When E6018 was delivered on 6 February 1966 it was with small yellow warning panels, however, it was soon to emerge from Eastleigh Works with wrap around full yellow ends and its numbers moved to behind the cab doors in February/March 1967. Here she is at St.Denys with the 08.45 from Waterloo on 17 June 1967, the Class 73 seems to have been repainted again conventionally in 1968. *John H.Bird/www.Anistr.com*

All of these electro-diesels were allocated when new to Stewarts Lane, although numbers E6007 to E6028 would be re-allocated to 70D Eastleigh for a short while from July 1967 until June 1968, otherwise during the period covered by this book they were all based at Stewarts Lane. In our first view of E6042 working along with E6048 on a heavy track maintenance train at Glynde on a Sunday in April 1968, all looks well and as it should be. *Peter Simmonds*

Tucked away out of sight on 18 December 1968 we see the now battered E6042 after a mishap. Another of the class in a spot of bother the same year was E6023 off the road at Earley on 26 April.
Both: Andy Gibbs Collection

Opposite: A lunchtime visit to Hither Green one day in August 1968 produces this duo of E6036 and E6038 stabled outside in the shed yard.
Strathwood Library Collection

Having been recently repainted E6009 passes Northam conveying H.M. The Queen and the Duke of Edinburgh from Waterloo to Southampton Docks to view the transatlantic liner, Queen Elizabeth II, on 1 May 1969, the day before the great ship's maiden voyage to New York.
John H. Bird/www.Anistr.com

A favourite place for your author both after school and throughout lunch breaks during his school years was the level crossing here at Wood Lane between Isleworth and Syon Lane stations on the Hounslow loop. On this occasion, we see E6024 with an up goods on 25 July 1969. *John Scrace*

Opposite: During late 1969 and into 1970 a few of the Class 73s headed back northwards to be overhauled at Crewe Works such as E6015 seen here. Another example was the ill-fated E6027 which would be destroyed in the crash at Horsham on 9 January 1972, although one cab was saved and later fitted to repair E6001. *Strathwood Library Collection*

We can enjoy a second look at E6012, this time ex-works in the carriage sidings at Clapham Junction resplendent in its shiny new paint in September 1969. Also in view are an ex-works Class 33 and a 4-COR coupled to an early blue liveried example standing on the Windsor lines. *Rail Photoprints*

Our final view of a Class 73 for this volume is also a sad one as E6040 was rostered to assist in the Farewell to the Southern BILs railtour on 25 September 1971 here at Twickenham, the 2-BIL units used were 2135, 2111 and 2140. *Rail Photoprints*

Class 74

A line up of at least four redundant Class 71 locomotives are in the process of conversion into Class 74 electro-diesels in this scene during a Sunday enthusiast visit to the main erecting shops at Crewe Works on 19 March 1967. *John Green/Strathwood Library Collection*

The first to be completed was E6101 which had originally been E5015, it was seen at various locations within Crewe Works for several months during 1967 before it was released finally to traffic on 11 February 1968. The first into service officially was E6102 on 5 November 1967, they were all sent to Stewarts Lane when new for crew training although they were allocated to Eastleigh. *Strathwood Library Collection*

Although this shot at Clapham Junction is undated we can surmise it be very soon after E6109's entry into service which was on 28 April 1968. Renumbering of the entire class into TOPS was carried out between December 1973 and February 1974, with E6109 becoming 74009 in January 1974.
Rail Online

The first to be withdrawn of the ten converted electro-diesels in Class 74 was 74006 on 20 June 1976 due to accident damage, next to go was 74002 in June 1977, this left the eight remaining locomotives to all face withdrawal as of 31 December 1977. As we see E6101 at Clapham Junction in September 1969, we are reminded their careers were very short indeed. *Rail Online*